Midwest Musings

poems by

Heather D. Frankland

Finishing Line Press
Georgetown, Kentucky

Midwest Musings

Copyright © 2023 by Heather D. Frankland
ISBN 979-8-88838-383-4 First Edition
All rights reserved under International and Pan-American Copyright Conventions. No part of this book may be reproduced in any manner whatsoever without written permission from the publisher, except in the case of brief quotations embodied in critical articles and reviews.

ACKNOWLEDGMENTS

I would like to acknowledge and thank the literary journals and presses for publishing the following poems:

Plane Tree Journal—"Down by the White River"
Ice Cube Press—"Hoarder"
New Purlieu Review—"A Gathering"
Tall Grass Guild—"Taming the Rain" previously published as, "Thunder"

Publisher: Leah Huete de Maines
Editor: Christen Kincaid
Cover Art: Tina Browder
Author Photo: Jay Hemphill
Cover Design: Elizabeth Maines McCleavy

Order online: www.finishinglinepress.com
also available on amazon.com

Author inquiries and mail orders:
Finishing Line Press
PO Box 1626
Georgetown, Kentucky 40324
USA

Table of Contents

A Country Kitchen Window 1

A Big Fish 3

The Luna Moth 4

Stillness 5

Absence 6

Still-life 9

Down by the White River 10

Hoarder 11

Agency 12

The Next Dance 14

You Are This Picture, Cropped Out 16

Chicago Romance 17

Family Quilt 18

Grandma's House 19

Taming the Rain 20

A Gathering 21

Even the Air Feels Green 23

This chapbook is dedicated to my family.

A Country Kitchen Window
to Grandma Frankland

Wooden frame, two sun catchers cascade
rainbows across my face as I pretend that I like washing dishes,
submerging my hands into the sudsy water, seeing bubbles
on my pale, wrinkling skin. My ring (no wedding ring)
is placed by the Yardley English Lavender bottle,
something so simple and so elegant.

All of us female relatives no longer ask to help
we say—*sit down, Grandma, and relax*
still she runs around to make sure
everything is okay; everyone is okay,
fluttering from person to person
like a butterfly dancing among stalks of milkweed.

Yet, there are stories beyond the sweetness
you associate with a grandmother:

An Easter chick ripped open by the dog,
my uncle as a young boy crying,
Grandma taking out her thread, steadily,
stuffing the organs back in,
sewing the chick back together.
The chick lived to be an old chicken, my dad remembers

I am not as strong of a woman as Grandma, still
I can wash dishes and watch bluebirds, as bright as figurines
you see in the store windows, fly to their nest,
race to build a home and family
before the invasive English sparrows
smother their happiness again.

Can the domestic also be the heroic?
Can the ordinary also be the extraordinary?
I think, my dishwater, wrinkled hands tell me of stories
I have yet to translate,
I have yet (and perhaps never) to find the right words.

On the Line by Tina Browder

A Big Fish

A goldfish, a feeder fish given a chance to be a family pet
swam as if it knew us—Peaches and Cream—I named it,
would follow us from one side of the aquarium to the next
its open 0 of a mouth always rhythmic, always hungry
it would grow as big as this tank, if we let it, it would grow
as big as the puddle outside, the pond, it would be a magic fish
growing as big as my 8-year old hand, and then it would be special—
worthy of a family tour—there is the bathroom, and here in the back
bedroom, the goldfish. I could imagine my friends
staring at the goldfish
its eyes bigger than their eyes. *We may have a small house*, I'd say,
but we have a big fish. By then I would have conversations
with the fish—we'd blink messages, jokes, stories.
I could teach it tricks, and it would dazzle the neighborhood kids.
This cool girl and her forever-clever fish—they'd say in awe.
I'd be in the newspaper, page 1 or 2, my fish and me.
But supposedly, it wasn't smart, its waste
trailing and clouding up the aquarium, and in the end
that was the reason that the neighbors told us it died.
Peaches and Cream too big to be flushed down the drain
yet too small to merit a grave, went to the creek,
the land of blue herons and crawdads,
the land of mud and forgotten wishes,
where there were not enough dandelion promises
to make that fish fly.

The Luna Moth

Whoever thought moths were dour women in long nightgowns,
hems collecting dust from corners, faces defined by shadows, was wrong,
and never knew the luna moth.

You and I and the luna moth were friends,
night pressed its hand on our skin
and you and I breathed deeply—
jasmine grew between our tongues.

One night on one of our walks, I spotted
our luna moth in the parking lot, wounded, missing a leg,
balancing like a crippled dancer.
We watched her wobble, dodge one headlight
after another, leaving crumbs of herself behind.

Grabbing a branch, I waited
until the moth crawled on, and I could put her somewhere soft.
You told me you'd check on her in the morning,
as she stumbled into the shadows, you drew circles on my back
whispered that we should go.
And I left that luna moth, wounded and alone.

The luna moth lost more legs, I believe,
she was found by a child who enjoyed pulling her apart.
He painted the walls with her wings, smeared that green fabric
over his mouth, left the rest in the toilet
where she dissolved like single-sheeted toilet paper.

And where were you? Were you watching?
The moth is dead, and although I don't know if it was your fault
or mine, I know it is dead, and that is all there is to say.
The open O of our mouths leaked out wingless luna moths,
twigs with eyes, then ants, then mosquitoes,
then flies, until there was only air—
distance, space, and patches of memory between us.

Stillness

In this yellow kitchen of broken tiles, dried raisins and dust
mingle under the heavy fridge. Mom's swollen fingers wash
the dishes. The suds on her fingers would look lovely if they didn't
cause skin to wrinkle. The diamond on her wedding ring
would look fragile if I didn't know that it cracked glass.

And I, a girl, who thinks too much, escape to the bedroom.
Cicadas sing their small death chants—hum and crescendo—
wax poetic about the heroes and the heroines they expect
in their mates. They chatter the whole night, gossip
like young girls standing in front of bathroom mirrors at school
dances.

I hear the owls. I hear the katydids. I see glimmers of lightning
bug fire. Trains howl to each other in the night. The heavy air
fingers through my curtains. And still, I am lonely in this little
room, the wood floor, cold on my feet.

Absence

*I can't believe you
call this a creek,*
my friend, Steve, had said,
it's more like a ditch.

I once saw
a blue heron
on this creek.
I couldn't tell what it was
until it covered the sky
with its wings.

There was a small family
of willows on one bank—
their long manes dragged
across the dirt
creating patterns
waves and severed lines.

On the other side
were wildflowers.
Grandma marveled at the colors:
Queen Anne's lace, bluebells,
goldenrod, morning glories, and daisies,
amazed that we could have
such a collection in the city.

In spring to early summer
aisles of ducklings
followed their mallard mother
as she swam away from every human form
and hid in the long grass.

A strange island
extended a small hand
to the mainland.
And I remember the challenge
of jumping across stones to where
the mud would hug
my white tennis shoes.

And now. . .
Dad and I walk on uneven ground.
The island has been gutted and gulped
by hungry machines,
and the willows are stumps.

With an order to clean the creek,
the city planned to rip all the trees out
of their sockets, clear the bank,
make nature nice and orderly
sterile like a hospital.
Mom called and complained,
and sugar babies were planted
for public relations.

I close my eyes
and picture a naked creek,
thin water running
through the callused,
hairless limbs, Nair applied
and burning its long legs.
The animals—ghosts,
the stumps—tombs,
and me—waiting
for my blue heron to fly.

Landscape by Tina Browder

Still Life

Outside from this stairwell where we sit
to wait out the rain,
there is a woods next to a coal factory
and one deer prancing through a block of green
leaves pressed against fence posts and telephone wires.

The city will say not to feed her,
that even a doe can get aggressive.
Children will try to touch her—
hold out their hands,
pretend they have something inside.

If she leaves from what-seems-safe
leaping from the fenced-in woods to a neighboring yard
full of budding flowers and young branches,
the city will deport her in the morning
to a place where hunting season is more frequent.

But for now, the doe is in her woods,
and we are here pressed tight.
The smell of fresh rain slips through the door—
the howling of the wind stalled on the other side.
We can't change her fate. We don't even try.
We can't even think of what happens when we leave this shelter—

the rain makes us stay, we will tell anyone who asks,
the rain makes us stay longer than intended—
you touch a raindrop on my skin, and I pretend
that I don't know that we won't last
much longer than this storm
and so we sit in this stairwell,
and the doe paces in her woods—
safe for now.

Down by the White River

Down by the White River, we watch mermaids lounge their mildewed bodies on couches cast off, plaid, ripped, ripples of white stuffing barely clinging to rusted wires.

The mermaids sing but they are not their siren sisters; their voices grab a melody and then fall flat. Someone says that it could be the pollution, batteries left on the banks of the White River, the city roping off sections, telling children to be careful

But we adults, we gather and gawk at the mermaids, chart their changing skin, their stench, their teeth hanging by small threads.
We see how our White River, once white and always called white, turns sewage gray and brown.

The current is small; the stolen bicycle, grass clippings, beer cans, cigarette ashes form an island around the mermaids. One—the only one who bares any resemblance to her former self—pulls out a love note from a bottle wedged between rock and plastic, *I'll grant you your wish, my darling*, she sings.

I see you edge away; was it the love note you wrote last spring to her when her eyes were clear, her hair that fairytale yellow, and you believed that loving a magical being made you magical?

Where, where is he that desires me? She sings, *Where, where is he?*
And those clear blues you once praised? Slime clogged, and thankfully, she never saw you walk away.

Hoarder

I collected your love declaration in this old mason jar
bought from a yard sale of neighbors I never met
until they were leaving.

I capped it tightly—your, "I love you,"
forgot about it for months until the cat almost knocked it over
stretching past plants to reach sunlight.

If only it could bloom into your tongue,
then your face, and your body.

If only, I could can you like garden tomatoes
or green beans, lima beans, peaches
store you in the kitchen cupboard
for the winter months when the sunlight
fades at five o'clock and I hide myself
in layers against the chill.

Agency

I am not what you want:
a porcelain model that says yes
an exotic Barbie doll that specializes
in sex toys, sex tapes, and barbed wire.
I am a girl hiding in a field
I am studying toads, which ones hop
the furthest away from their homes.

When we met, I was coy
mouth painted red hot pink
spicy smiles and licking of lips
it was Halloween; every day is Halloween
acting the parts we think we play well.

But I am a girl hiding in a field
ear pressed to the ground
looking for grasshoppers, counting crickets
collecting notes to create a mixture of sounds.

When you looked at me, you imagined
foreign words crawling and covering yours
or me silent and handling you, whatever you needed
you called, I came, you asked, I acted, you thought
I was a photo of your past, pressed to your covers
features almost erased by the sweat of your hands.

But I am a girl hiding in the field
I am creating a map of the best places to hide
behind the tall grass, near the fairy's mound
under the old oak tree, by the robin's nest
I leave notes to myself to follow myself back
You zoomed past with someone else in your passenger side,
someone else smiling, crossing her legs, licking her lips

It had to be someone else
for I am a girl hiding in the field
I know where the best flowers grow
I know where the rabbits hide their young
and the deer tiptoe past hunters' bow.
I know how to catch fireflies
Sing them a song and wait.
I know where the wishes blow.
Yes, even this, I know.

The Next Dance

The lovely girls in their dresses,
satin colorful and stiff like tulips
announcing the start of spring,
play with their fancy socks
and borrowed necklaces
at the back of the school dance.

But the boys only show
their dance moves outside
in the parking lot
they spin in circles
near the playground
where swings sway
by themselves
as if bodies
were inside them,
first anchoring down,
then giving in.
The body without knowing
already knows the beat.

Within by Tina Browder

You Are This Picture, Cropped Out
For Mike

I imagine smoke clouds
similar to the city's firework display
where I used to jump to see spider webs
lace fingers with our dying elms' branches
while you joked with my dad,
and my mother's ice cubes clinked
bells in a nearly empty glass.

Scattered over the narrow creek bed
by a hill, downward sloop, long grass green,
near two gardens heavy with tomato girth
and jailed green beans climbing,
it is here that you rest
by the many stones to jump across and reach the other side.
Here, where you used to complain
about the beavers clogging up the drain.
Here, where I would think about that fireplace
inside crackling wood and the smell of smoke
carried home on my clothes through the dark roads
with an empty pot steadied between my feet.

I hear it took a while to set you free,
you sifted through that creek's current,
clung to wet rocks and fish scales, remained
there to watch your widow curled on your side of the bed
near the video tapes where you collected us,
but we never collected you.
Six months, what preparation?
Hope clogged our brains.
The rolls are blank.

Chicago Romance

There are nights when the sky looks so dark it makes
Lake Michigan drown out our heavens and stars.
I stand close enough that I can see you slip in,
jagged stone bleeding, kicked in ribs,
until you submit and become, to my shore,
the smooth candied glass I can collect
and put next to my bed.

I dream of sweaty looks between strangers—
cheap newspaper ink smeared
on fingertips and cheekbones
and buildings that scrape
their length against open sky,
gagging the moon.

In this city, painted murals stretch
their bodies against subway walls
and a street musician sings Marvin Gaye
to puzzle-pieces of missed connections
who leave the EL with their own music
crammed in their solitary ears.

Although headlights can create fireflies
out of shards of glass on cracked concrete
and make them look like something
I would want to wear on my wedding finger,
cardboard boxes fill what is left of me:
torn advertisements wrap around
the things that might break in transit.

But you, this stone, you are already broken,
and through you I can't see
stars lingering in Lake Michigan
no matter how hard I squint and wish
someone loved me at least this month,
loved me enough to pause my packing
and persuade me to stay.

Family Quilt

Open veiled branches
lean into the wind
so that I can hear them beyond the screen door
clicking messages I feel humming in my bones,
the green sticky, the deep burst of breath,
and finally rain so thick,
I can't see my hands
in front of my face.

This knows me.

Hollow branches snap, I am
underneath the sky
only windows and a door
even when voiceless
and stunned by lightning
even when hidden
and dreaming of drought
even when drenched
and paper-molded
even after the soft oak is struck dead
and the gutter fills with someone else's wishes
even after the green is not quite home anymore—

This still knows me, will always know me
it welcomes me back
no matter how many times
I promise good-bye.

Grandma's House
    for Grandma Malone

At Grandma's house,
the screen door swings
and catches.
Its sound—
breaks me.
Grandma's not on the other side.
Walk to the hallway.
Control the lion
in my throat.
Swallow the food
left for us.

The house feels like her.
Told to look
through her things—
The letters I wrote her
when I was a kid.
The Czech tale I shared.
The pictures.
The music box
Mom saved for me,
the report card.

The house smells
like Grandma.
Step outside.
The fields.
The yard where we
cousins played ball.
Bases made of trees
and broken frisbees.
Those summer visits.
Grandma watched
on the front porch swing.
Iced tea in hand, sweet.
Laughter. So much laughter.
Gone. Quiet.
Quietly gone.

Taming the Rain

I will tame the rain one day I will
teach it tricks how to
stand on my shoulder or inner lip.
It will be a tendril curling
across my palm or a dot
of sweat sifting through my hair.
It will be my party trick
when the stars think they're going to shine
when the moon thinks it'll be praised
I'll draw the rain out. I'll have a code word
for a little rain, average rain, and a Midwestern storm.
The weather guys will be confused in
how those orange areas splatter
so easily on their screen.
I will not warn.
I will not tell those I love.
I will not.
The storm will come and wash out
all the oils on the highway—
a skeleton concrete clean drifting.
You'll see after the rain is tamed.
I'll drench you awake.

A Gathering

Grandma planted this thistle, those peonies, lilacs, tulips,
daffodils, and money plants.

We cup our palms over seeds and dig-up old bulbs.
These belong home. Home has become someplace else.

If there were roses, we would take a branch. If there were daisies,
we'd place them in a vase over the table, with water
and a half teaspoon of sugar to sustain their death-life.

I see smashed clover, headless dandelions, and creeping charlies
void of purple trumpet mouths.

I want those, too.

This dirt is loose. Peek—there is a foundation left of the house.

Can I take that splintered wood? Can I take that old shovel?

Under the lilac bush there is a broken mouthful.

Jaw, where is the jaw, the femur, the toenails thick thin brittle?

There is a body in there. I am sure.

Rich earthworm dirt diet of a family.

Could it be the stillborn child or the imaginary friends
or the family dog or the boarder?

Could the ghosts package their selves in dirt,

wading in waist length weeds and grime?

I want some of that.

There must be something of me in here.

An earring, an eyelash, an expression borrowed.

Could it be the shoulder bones or the shape of the face?

Could it be under the dogwood trees
and the one blind crab apple tree?

Quick, take it all before it can all be taken back.

Even the Air Feels Green

Even the air feels green, the trees with leaves like letters home
Don't you see it anymore, the green? There are lilacs in his yard
carrot greens, bunches of herbs that are bunches, not the few strands
I call a small bunch in the Southwest. I remember one day,
I planted parsley, and in that one day after planting,
I said good-bye to parsley.
In the Midwest, the Southwest seems like a fairytale,
a place of big landscapes.

Some mornings, I tell my Midwestern
friends and family, I smell campfire
Some mornings, I can see pyres of smoke burning our Gila forest.
Some mornings when the window is left open,
I swear I left the oven on—I look, check,
make sure that nothing is burning, but of course it's burning
it's all burning outside—we're ants under this huge glass.
Here I have this meager-excuse of a garden,
this well-earned excuse of a garden
the trial and error, the volume-planting, and the amazing discovery
that every single snapdragon planted survived,
the wishing that every single snapdragon planted didn't survive
so that I'd have a place to put the tomatoes,
to give them the space to pretend
that they can become like their Midwestern cousins—endless.

Don't you see the green, anymore? I tell him
while looking up at the Midwestern trees
tall and abundant, the lilac bush scarcely tended or watered,
the milkweed, the grass without goat-heads;
I could walk barefoot on this grass,
I could feel the dirt between my toes, and it would be cool.
But I no longer saw the green when I grew-up here either—
I didn't notice it beyond the springtime
when the winter make us sick of monochrome.
I didn't notice how soft the grass was or how plentiful the garden
or how the soil actually looked like black gold—rather than

being purchased from a company called Black & Gold.
I didn't notice the tiny buttercups by the woods or the bees
so full of clover that they seemed to nap on yards, only startling
when children came by or dogs or lawn mowers. No, I didn't notice—

I forgot to notice, and it makes me wonder what am I forgetting now
in this Southwestern land of big landscapes, in this large state
of diverse places. Am I forgetting you, the desert willow,
or you, the alligator juniper that makes me sneeze,
when I look out and see charred remains, is there anything
that I'll remember, anything that I can put back together
or at least, remember enough to mourn its sudden loss?

With Thanks

I am grateful to Tina Browder and her amazing artwork. Thank you for letting me include a few of your pieces.

I would also like to acknowledge and thank various people and places who have supported my creative work over the years, some of who read various versions of these poems. Thank you to Mom, Dad, Erich, Tammy, Aaron, Nicole, and the rest of the family; thank you to friends near and far—Tina Browder, Melanie Sweeney Bowen, Andrea Crain, Jay Wartenberg, Carla Criscuolo, Gayle Perez, Elysia Mbuja, Emma Adams, Marci Tipton, Katharine Perez Lockett, Margaret Claire Cunningham, Lizzie Moran, Daniel Alkov, Jeanne Tenorio, Meghan Wilbar, Miguel De La Cruz, Julia Smith, Jennifer Johnston, and Dara Naphan-Kingery; and thank you to writers' groups, programs, and professors who have been supportive and made me awaken as a poet—Beth Ann Fennelly, cin salach, Marge Piercy and the Marge Piercy Poetry Intensive Workshop 2022 poets, Knox College, New Mexico State University MFA program, Silver City River Poets, Shut Up! and Write Group, and Western New Mexico University.

Originally from Muncie, Indiana, **Heather Frankland** currently lives in Silver City, NM where she teaches English Composition at Western New Mexico University. She holds both a Masters of Public Health and a Masters of Fine Arts in Poetry from New Mexico State University and a BA in Creative Writing with a Concentration in Environmental Studies from Knox College. She served as a Peace Corps and Peace Corps Response Volunteer in Peru and Panama.

Heather finds herself intrigued by landscapes and the role they can play in language, story, and poetry. A frequent traveler, Heather has lived in landscapes as varied as the Pacific Northwest to the Southwest to South America. However, no matter where she lives, she carries the Midwest with her and that sense of home. This chapbook is dedicated to where it all began—when a backyard felt like a world, where the thunderstorms ignited creativity, and how the trains seemed to call to each other in the middle of the night when they crossed Muncie on their way to somewhere else.

Luckily, she has been supported by family, friends, professors, and wonderful opportunities. In the summer of 2022, she attended Marge Piercy's Intensive Poetry Workshop, an experience that was supportive, encouraging, and long-lasting. Heather has been published in *ROAR, Plane Tree Journal, Sin Fronteras Press, Sweet Lit, Slippery Elm Literary Journal*, and others. She writes poetry, fiction, and creative nonfiction. Currently, she is working on a couple projects in each.

www.ingramcontent.com/pod-product-compliance
Lightning Source LLC
Chambersburg PA
CBHW040308170426
43194CB00022B/2944